PRIMARY SOURCES OF AMERICAN WARS™

The Civil War

Georgene Poulakidas

The Rosen Publishing Group's
PowerKids Press™
PRIMARY SOURCE

Published in 2006 by The Rosen Publishing Group, Inc.
29 East 21st Street, New York, NY 10010

First Edition

Editor: Eric Fein
Book Design: Erica Clendening
Photo Researcher: Jeff Wendt

Photo Credits: Cover, p. 18 (top) © Hulton/Archive/Getty Images; pp. 4 (top), 6 (bottom), 8 (top), 10, 12, 16, 18 (bottom), 20 Library of Congress, Prints and Photographs Division; p. 4 (bottom) © Corbis; p. 6 (top) National Archives and Records Administration; pp. 8 (bottom), 14 (bottom) Library of Congress, Geography and Map Division; p. 14 (top) Library of Congress, Manuscript Division.

Library of Congress Cataloging-in-Publication Data

Poulakidas, Georgene.
 The Civil War / Georgene Poulakidas.— 1st ed.
  p. cm. — (Primary sources of American wars)
 Includes index.
 Contents: One country, two ways of life — Slavery and states' rights — War! — The first battle of Bull Run — The North and South on the move — The South goes North — Taking the South — The final blow — The results of the war.
 ISBN 1-4042-2684-2 (lib. bdg.)
 1. United States—History—Civil War, 1861-1865—Juvenile literature. [1. United States—History—Civil War, 1861-1865.] I. Title. II. Series.

 E468.P68 2006
 973.7—dc22

                                        2003026024

Manufactured in the United States of America

To my sister Jennifer

Contents

At the time of the Civil War, the South's economy was based largely on agriculture. New Orleans, Louisiana (left), was an important port from which many crops grown in the South were shipped.

One Country, Two Ways of Life

The American **Civil War** was the result of a series of disagreements and differences between the Northern and Southern states of the United States. Northern states were becoming **industrialized**. The North needed roads, railroads, and canals to move their goods. The North also wanted high taxes placed on goods from other countries. This would encourage Americans to buy goods made in the North.

The South's **economy** was mainly based on farming and slave labor. Slaves were used to harvest the crops and work the farms and plantations. The South wanted low taxes so it could trade its crops for cheap European goods.

■ *By the mid-eighteenth century, many parts of the North had become industrialized. Factories, such as this one in New Hampshire, were common sights in cities and towns throughout the region.*

The Compromise Act of 1850 (left) was one of several attempts by the U.S. Congress to deal with the issue of slavery. In part, the act provided that California would be admitted to the Union as a non-slave state and that New Mexico and Utah would be admitted as states with the issue of slavery to be decided later.

Slavery and States' Rights

By the early 1800s, many Northerners began to believe that slavery was wrong. They did not want slavery to be allowed in the new states that were joining the **Union**. The subject of states' rights was another point that divided the North and the South. The North wanted a strong **federal** government that would build roads and railroads and pass high taxes.

The South feared that a federal government that was too strong would make laws to stop slavery. For over 40 years, the U.S. Congress had tried to find a way to deal with the question of slavery. Nothing seemed to satisfy both the Northern and Southern states. With anger building on both sides, it appeared that the country was headed for war.

- *People in the United States were sharply divided on the issue of slavery, even in the North. Pennsylvania Hall in Philadelphia was the home of the Abolition Society, a group working to end slavery. On May 17, 1838, a band of pro-slavery forces burned down the building in anger.*

■ Southern forces fired the first shots of the Civil War on April 12, 1861. At dawn, they began bombarding Fort Sumter, a federal fort in South Carolina.

War!

The election of Abraham Lincoln as president angered the South. Lincoln was opposed to slavery. Weeks later, the Southern state of South Carolina **seceded**, or withdrew, from the Union. Other states seceded too. In February 1861, these states formed a new independent government called the **Confederate States of America.**

Lincoln warned the South that the federal government would protect its property in the South. However, on April 12, 1861, Confederate forces **bombarded** Fort Sumter, a federal fort in the harbor of Charleston, South Carolina. The attack ended any hope of peace. Two days later, federal troops in the fort **surrendered.** The Civil War had begun. Lincoln asked the Northern states to supply 75,000 troops for the war. Jefferson Davis, president of the Confederate States, asked for 200,000 troops.

■ *This 1862 map is colored to show free, or non-slave states (pink), border slave states (yellow), and Confederate, or seceded, states (green).*

BURNSIDE'S
BRIGADE
BULL RUN.

BURNSIDE'S
BRIGADE
BULL RUN.

COL. BURNSIDE'S BRIGADE FIRST AND SECOND RHODE ISLAND, AND SEVENTY-FIRST NEW YORK REGIMENTS, WITH THEIR ARTILLERY, ATTACKING THE REBEL BATTERIES AT BULL RUN

This 1861 print (left) shows Union forces in action at the First Battle of Bull Run.

The First Battle of Bull Run

The first important battle of the Civil War took place in Manassas, Virginia, near a stream called Bull Run. The First Battle of Bull Run was fought on July 21, 1861. Union troops, led by General Irvin McDowell, attacked Confederate forces gathered around the town of Manassas, which was about 25 miles (40 km) from Washington, D.C.

The Confederate troops turned back the Union attack. A shocked Union army was sent running back to nearby Washington, D.C. The First Battle of Bull Run showed that the Union was ill prepared for war. Southern soldiers, many of them with hunting experience, were more skilled at firing guns than the Union army. The South easily won the battle. Many people believe that the South could have won the war by following the Union army into Washington, D.C., and defeating them there.

■ *This photo was taken after the fighting at Bull Run. Notice the destroyed bridge in the center of the photo.*

The Virginia (at right in image) was made from the remains of a Confederate ship called the Merrimack. After the battle, Confederate forces destroyed it. This kept it from being taken by the Union.

The North and South on the Move

In February 1862, General Ulysses S. Grant led Union forces in the capture of two Confederate forts in Tennessee. In April, Union troops won the Battle of Shiloh. These victories gave the North a **foothold** in the South.

In March 1862, the Confederates attacked the Union navy at Hampton Roads, Virginia, at the mouth of the James River. A Confederate **ironclad** ship, the *Virginia*, was met by a Union ironclad, the *Monitor*. The two ships furiously battled to a draw. The battle proved that ironclad ships would soon replace each navy's wooden vessels.

On September 17, 1862, the Battle of Antietam was fought in Maryland. Confederate general Robert E. Lee was hoping to win an important battle in Union **territory**. However, Lee's forces were defeated. Over 11,000 men were killed or wounded in the fighting.

■ *The Confederate army began the Battle of Shiloh (left) with a sneak attack on Union forces. The Union, however, managed a strong counterattack and drove the Confederates back.*

In November 1863, President Lincoln gave a speech at the Gettysburg battlefield. Known as the Gettysburg Address (handwritten copy at left) it explained his hopes to bring the nation back together again.

The South Goes North

On July 1 to July 3, 1863, one of the most famous battles in U.S. history was fought in Gettysburg, Pennsylvania. Confederate general Robert E. Lee pushed far into Union territory, hoping to win a major battle in the North. For three days, fierce fighting took place, and casualties on both sides were very high. On July 3, the Confederates launched a final attack, which they hoped would win the battle. Known as Pickett's Charge, the assault was met head-on by Union forces and driven back.

The defeated Confederate forces retreated, but were not chased by the Union army. President Lincoln was angered by the wasted opportunity to end the war that was tearing the nation apart.

■ *This 1863 print is a view of the Gettysburg battlefield, showing the positions of the Union and Confederate armies.*

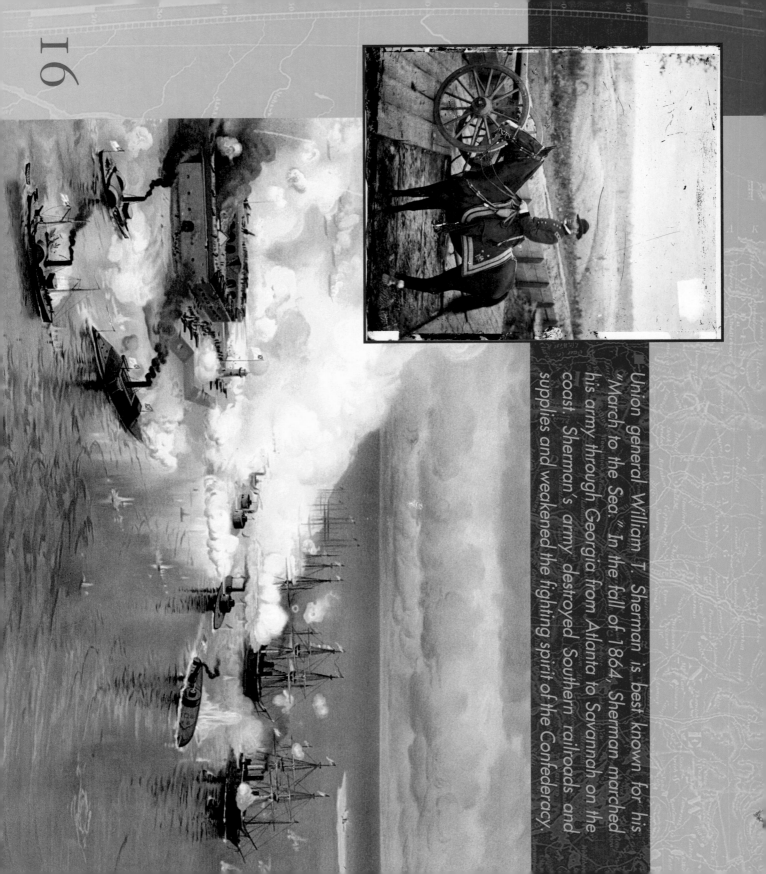

Union general William T. Sherman is best known for his "March to the Sea." In the fall of 1864, Sherman marched his army through Georgia from Atlanta to Savannah on the coast. Sherman's army destroyed Southern railroads and supplies and weakened the fighting spirit of the Confederacy.

Taking the South

On March 9, 1864, President Lincoln put General Ulysses S. Grant in charge of the Union army. For the first time since the start of the war, Lincoln believed he had the right person leading the army.

On June 20, Grant's troops surrounded Confederate forces led by General Lee at Petersburg, Virginia. Grant decided to starve the Confederates into surrendering. This **siege** lasted for almost a year.

On August 5, 1864, the Union navy took control of Mobile Bay, Alabama. This further weakened the South.

The Union continued to move deep into the South. In November and December 1864, Union general William T. Sherman led about 65,000 troops through Georgia, taking control of it. He then marched on to South Carolina and North Carolina. From there, he headed to meet Grant in Virginia.

■ *Union admiral David Farragut gained control of the port city of Mobile Bay, Alabama, in August 1864. With Mobile Bay in Union hands, the South was unable to bring in much-needed supplies through the city.*

17

On April 9, 1865, General Lee (center, seated at left) surrendered to General Grant (center, seated at right) at Appomattox Court House, Virginia. The surrender ended four years of bloody battle.

The Final Blow

Sherman's march through the South crushed Southern hopes of winning the war. It was only a matter of time before the Union army would defeat its enemy.

The end came when Grant managed to cut off the two railroads that had been supplying the Confederates in Petersburg and Richmond, Virginia. On April 2, 1865, Grant's forces were able to break through Lee's lines in Petersburg. This was followed by several days of fierce fighting. Finally, Grant sent Lee a letter asking him to surrender. Lee wrote back, asking for surrender terms. On April 9, the two generals met at a house in the village of Appomattox Court House, Virginia. There, Lee surrendered to Grant. Grant treated Lee and his men with respect. The Confederates were allowed to keep their horses and officers were allowed to keep their handguns.

■ *Petersburg, Virginia, was an important point for the defense of the Confederate capital of Richmond. In April 1865, Union forces (left) drove the Confederate army from the city. Several days later, Lee surrendered to Grant at Appomattox Court House.*

To celebrate the end of the war, President Lincoln (left) went to see a play at Ford's Theatre on the night of April 14. It was there that John Wilkes Booth shot him. The assassin was shot and killed twelve days later.

The Results of the War

However, misfortune struck just days later. On April 14, President Lincoln was assassinated in Washington, D.C. The **assassin**, John Wilkes Booth, was a Confederate **supporter**. Many Northerners wanted to strike at the South for the murder of Lincoln. However, no action was taken, and by May 26, the last of the Confederate forces surrendered.

American society was forever changed by the war. Over 600,000 people died in the fighting. Bitterness about the war remained on both sides. There were also questions about how to fit the newly freed slaves into everyday life. The future was filled with uncertainty. However the Union's victory established that no state had the right to end the Union. The United States of America would remain united.

- *Many Southern cities were badly destroyed during the four years of fighting. This photo was taken in Charleston, South Carolina, in April 1865.*

Timeline

Early 1800s Congress tries to deal with the issue of slavery.

1860 Abraham Lincoln is elected president of the United States. South Carolina secedes from the Union. Other Southern states soon follow.

April 1861 Confederate forces attack Fort Sumter in Charleston, South Carolina. Federal troops surrender the fort.

July 1861 The First Battle of Bull Run is fought.

February 1862 Union forces capture two forts in Tennessee.

March 1862 The *Virginia* and the *Monitor* battle to a draw near Chesapeake Bay.

September 17, 1862 Union forces win the Battle of Antietam.

July 1-3, 1863 The South loses the Battle of Gettysburg.

March 1864 Lincoln puts General Ulysses S. Grant in charge of the entire Union army.

June 1864 The siege of Petersburg, Virginia, begins.

August 1864 Admiral David Farragut wins control of Mobile Bay, Alabama.

November 1864 General William Sherman begins his march through the South.

April 9, 1865 General Robert E. Lee surrenders to General Ulysses S. Grant at the village of Appomattox Court House, Virginia, ending the war.

April 14, 1865 President Lincoln is assassinated.

May 26, 1865 The last Confederate forces surrender to the Union.

Glossary

assassin (uh-SASS-ihn) A person who murders someone who is well known or important, such as a president.

bombarded (bom-BAHRD-ihd) To have attacked a place with heavy gunfire.

Civil War (SIV-il WOR) The war fought between the Confederacy, or Southern states, and the Union, or Northern states, that lasted from 1861–1865.

Confederate (kuhn-FED-ur-uht) Having to do with the Confederacy before and during the Civil War; someone who bands together with others for a common purpose.

economy (I-KON-uh-mee) The way a country runs its industry, trade, and finance.

federal (FED-ur-uhl) A government in which several states are united under and controlled by one central power or authority. However, each state also has its own government and can make its own laws.

foothold (FUT-hohld) A position usable as a base for further advance.

industrialized (in-DUHSS-tree-uh-lizd) To have set up businesses and factories in an area.

ironclad (EYE-urn-klad) A naval ship covered with iron, for protection against attacks.

retreated (ri-TREET-ihd) To have moved back or withdrawn from a difficult situation.

seceded (si-SEED-ihd) To have formally withdrawn from a group or an organization, often to form another organization.

siege (SEEJ) The surrounding of a place such as a castle or a city to cut off supplies and then wait for those inside to surrender.

supporter (suh-PORT-uhr) A person who believes in someone or favors something.

surrendered (suh-REN-durd) To have given up, or to have admitted, that you are beaten in a fight or battle.

territory (TER-uh-tor-ee) The land and waters under the control of a state, nation, or ruler.

Union (YOON-yuhn) The United States of America; the states that remained loyal to the federal government during the Civil War.

Index

Web Sites

Due to the changing nature of Internet links, PowerKids Press has developed an online list of Web sites related to the topic of this book. This site is updated regularly. Please use this link to access the list:

http://www.powerkidslinks.com/psaw/tcw/

Primary Sources

Cover: *The Battle of Antietam in Maryland,* 1862. Chromolithograph published by L. Prang & Co. [c. 1888]. Thure de Thulstrup, artist. Hulton/Archive. **Page 4 (inset):** *New Orleans from the lower cotton press,* 1852. Lithograph published by Smith Brothers & Co., 1852. David William Moody, artist. Library of Congress, Prints and Photographs Division. **Page 6 (inset):** *The Manchester Print Works Factory* [c. 1854]. **Page 6:** *The Compromise Act of 1850.* National Archives and Records Administration. **Page 6:** *Destruction by fire of Pennsylvania Hall, the new building of the Abolition Society, on the night of the 17th May, 1838.* Print, published 1838. Library of Congress, Prints and Photographs Division. **Page 8 (inset):** *Bombardment of Fort Sumter, Charleston Harbor, 12th & 13th of April, 1861.* Hand-colored lithograph by Currier & Ives [c. 1861]. Library of Congress, Prints and Photographs Division. **Page 8:** *Colton's new railroad & county map of the United States, the Canadas &c.* Published by J. H. Colton, 1862. Library of Congress, Geography and Map Division. **Page 10 (inset):** *Battle scenes, no. [Bull Run].* Hand-colored lithograph published at H. H. Lloyd & Co.'s [c. 1861]. Library of Congress Prints and Photographs Division. **Page 10:** *Cub Run, Va. View with destroyed bridge.* Glass stereograph by George N. Barnard, photographer, March 1862. Library of Congress, Prints and Photographs Division. **Page 12 (inset):** *Terrific combat between the "Monitor" 2 guns & Merrimac 10 guns.* Colored lithograph published by Currier & Ives [c. 1862]. Library of Congress, Prints and Photographs Division. **Page 12:** *The Battle of Shiloh.* Chromolithograph published by Prang & Co., c. 1888. Thure de Thulstrup, artist. Library of Congress, Prints and Photographs Division. **Page 14 (inset):** *Draft of the Gettysburg Address.* The Abraham Lincoln Papers at the Library of Congress, Manuscript Division. **Page 14:** *Gettysburg battlefield.* Color lithograph published by W. Endicott & Co. [c. 1863] John B. Bachelder, artist. Library of Congress, Geography and Map Division. **Page 16 (inset):** *Atlanta, Ga. Gen. William T. Sherman on horseback at Federal Fort No. 7.* Glass, wet collodion. Created by George N. Barnard, photographer [1864]. Library of Congress, Prints and Photographs Division. **Page 16:** *Battle of Mobile Bay.* Color lithograph [c. 1886]. Library of Congress, Prints and Photographs Division. **Page 18 (inset):** *The room in the McLean House, at Appomattox C.H., in which Gen. Lee surrendered to Gen. Grant.* Print [late nineteenth century]. Library of Congress, Prints and Photographs Division. **Page 18:** *Union soldiers in trenches before Petersburg.* Photographic print. Library of Congress, Prints and Photographs Division. **Page 20 (inset):** *Abraham Lincoln.* Photographic print, taken November 8, 1863. Alexander Gardner, photographer. Library of Congress, Prints and Photographs Division. **Page 20:** *Charleston, S.C. View of ruined buildings through porch of the Circular Church.* Glass stereograph. Published 1865. Library of Congress Prints and Photographs Division.